Cody Coyote Cooks!

A Southwest Cookbook

▼ ▲ ▼ ▲ ▼ ▲ ▼ ▲ ▼ ▲ ▼

For Kids

Denice Skrepcinski, Melissa T. Stock, and Lois Bergthold

Illustrations by Lois Bergthold

TRICYCLE PRESS
Berkeley, California

*Special thanks to Alyssa Skrepcinski,
kid editor and recipe tester. We would also like to thank
all the students who helped with the testing and retesting
of the recipes featured in this book, who provided us
with their appetites and honest evaluations.*

To Kelli and Sara Bergthold.

*And to Dave DeWitt,
whose wit, wisdom, and willingness
to share his talents have made
all of this possible.*

▽ ▲ ▽ ▲ ▽ ▲ ▽ ▲ ▽ ▲ ▽

TRICYCLE PRESS
P. O. Box 7123
Berkeley, California 94707

Distributed in Australia by E.J. Dwyer Pty., Ltd., in Canada by Publishers Group West, in New Zealand by Tandem Press, in South Africa by Real Books, and in the United Kingdom and Europe by Airlift Books.

Book design by Tasha Hall

Library of Congress Cataloging-in-Publication Data
Skrepcinski, Denice.
    Cody Coyote cooks!: a Southwest cookbook for kids / Denice Skrepcinski, Melissa T. Stock, and Lois Bergthold; illustrations by Lois Bergthold.
        p. cm.
    Includes index.
    Summary: Recipes with a Southwestern flavor, designed for children from ages six to eleven to prepare, are accompanied by several stories featuring the traditional trickster Coyote and several simple craft projects.
    ISBN 1-883672-37-6
    1. Cookery, American—Southwestern style—Juvenile literature. [1. Cookery, American—Southwestern style.] I. Stock, Melissa T. II. Bergthold, Lois. III. Title.
TX715.2.S69S57 1996
641.5979—dc20   96–10484
                                                                     CIP
                                                                     AC

Manufactured in Hong Kong

1 2 3 4 5 6 7 — 01 00 99 98 97 96

Contents

Introduction

Have you seen Coyote? Have you heard Coyote calling in the night? Have you followed Coyote's tracks through the southwestern sand? Have you wondered where he is going and what adventure he will have today?

The character Coyote is found in New Mexican stories, Native American legends, and cowboy tall tales. He is very clever and smart. Some stories tell of Coyote the trickster, challenging and trying to outsmart the other animals of the desert. He is very good at deceiving others. Coyote can also be very gullible, and because he has tricked many animals, he often gets tricked in return.

Many believe that the coyote has special powers. Indian legends tell of a magical coyote who helped create many of the things we have on Earth and in the sky. Stories of Coyote teach lessons of life to young Native Americans. In these legends Coyote is in constant motion, always looking over his shoulder, continuing his journey, always encountering different animals and humans who share his adventures.

Some of Cody Coyote's adventures in this book are based loosely on Native American legends, and some focus directly on the many cultural traditions represented throughout the West. Our hope is that in some small way, the adventures and recipes of Cody Coyote will better explain the many wonderful cuisines, cultures, and traditions that make the Southwest both mythical and magical.

Follow Coyote on his travels throughout the Southwest to see if today he is a clever hunter, a trickster, or a gullible fool. What adventures will he have? What animals and humans will he meet? What is he looking for?

FOR THE ADULT COYOTE
▽ ▲ ▽ ▲ ▽ ▲ ▽ ▲ ▲ ▽

Welcome to Cody Coyote's family guide to the Southwest. The legends and recipes will introduce your family to the wonderful cultures of the Southwest. Preparing food from the area is an exciting, hands-on adventure for your children. You'll be happy to know that the recipes in this book are not only fun and different, but are also kid tested and teacher approved! Children will love preparing them. It's a fun family activity, and best of all you get to eat the results!

As a parent, you know best what skills your child has and what he or she is capable of preparing in the kitchen. Cody's recipes have been tested by kids ages six to eleven, and the recipes are classified to help you decide which recipes to prepare and how much adult help is needed. One lizard means that the recipe is suitable for a beginner. Beginning recipes are simple; they require only a few ingredients and are easy to prepare. These would be best for younger children or for older children who want something easy or something that can be prepared in a shorter amount of time. The intermediate level is denoted with two lizards. These recipes require more dexterity in cutting, mixing, and preparation. Younger children can still do these with adult help. If you see three lizards, you'll know that the recipe is advanced. The advanced level is for older children or should be prepared with adult help.

Beginner

Intermediate

Advanced

Please preview the recipe your child wants to prepare to see if adult help is requested. Review the "Coyote caution" notes with your child before you prepare the recipe. They will give you safety tips you should be aware of when preparing the recipe.

Each recipe has an equipment list so that you can tell immediately what is needed. This way, you can screen recipes and select the ones your child is capable of preparing.

Most of the recipes serve four. They can easily be doubled if you need to serve more people or they can be cut in half if you are cooking for two.

Be sure to teach children good cooking habits now. Emphasize safety. Be sure your children are familiar with your kitchen, equipment, and utensils and know how to use them correctly. Use this chance to teach them about food safety and safe food handling. Be sure to include everyone in the cleanup; this is part of cooking. Cooking with children is very educational. They will learn about different cultures. They will also be learning reading and math skills, improving their manual dexterity, and more. Children really enjoy cooking and are very proud of their creations.

Many childhood memories are formed in the kitchen. These are times that the family creates together. We hope you'll use *Cody Coyote Cooks!* to create memories to share with your children.

COYOTE'S COOKING COMMANDMENTS

▽ ▲ ▽ ▲ ▽ ▲ ▽ ▲ ▲ ▽ ▲ ▽ ▲ ▽ ▲ ▽

1. Always check with a big coyote, an adult, before trying any recipes. Please get permission to cook and be sure an adult will be close. Never cook alone.

2. Read through the entire recipe before you do anything.

3. Make sure you'll have enough time to make the recipe and finish it. Remember to include cleanup time. It's frustrating if you start a recipe and are not be able to finish it.

4. Be sure to wash your hands thoroughly before you start to cook.

5. Assemble all the equipment and ingredients you will need *before* you start cooking.

6. Check the recipe to see if it requires adult coyote help. Be sure you ask for help with that part of the recipe. *Be safe!!*

7. Follow the directions in the order listed.

8. Clean up as you cook. Put things away as you use them, and rinse dishes and place them in the sink after you've used them. Mop up any messes or spills as soon as they happen. Be sure to pick up anything that drops on the floor; this could make the floor slippery.

9. Take care of all the appliances and equipment that you've used. Be sure to turn the oven off. If you've used a blender or other appliance, be sure it is cleaned off and put away.

10. Share your coyote creation with your family and friends. They will enjoy the results of your hard work. Eat and enjoy!

Coyote Cooking Terms

▽ ▲ ▽ ▲ ▽ ▲ ▽ ▲ ▲ ▽ ▲

bake: To cook food in an oven.

beat: To stir vigorously using a spoon or wire whisk.

blend: To make a mixture smooth. Ingredients should be mixed thoroughly by stirring or using a blender.

boil: To heat a liquid until it bubbles and the bubbles break on the surface of the liquid.

brown: To cook food until it is brown in color. When browning meat, meat should turn from pink or red to brown.

chop: To cut food into very small pieces.

cool: To let food sit after baking or cooking until it has cooled slightly or has come to room temperature.

dice: To cut food into small pieces (usually $1/4$ inch or smaller).

fry: To cook food in a frying pan while stirring it.

grate: To shred cheese by moving it downward against a grater.

grease: To cover the bottom of a baking dish or cookie sheet with shortening or butter. A pastry brush works best to do this.

knead: To take a ball of dough and push it away from you (on a floured surface), fold it over, and push again, repeating until the dough is flexible (as you would knead clay).

marinade: A sauce or liquid that food is placed in before cooking to flavor the food.

mix: To combine ingredients with a fork or spoon.

preheat: To set the oven temperature and turn it on before starting a recipe so the oven has time to heat up to the right temperature before you put food in the oven to bake. Ovens take about 10 minutes to preheat.

purée: To blend ingredients until they are smooth, with no lumps. You usually need a blender to make a purée.

roll out: To flatten dough using a rolling pin.

slice: To cut foods into thin pieces.

stir: To make circular movements with a fork or spoon to combine ingredients.

The Coyote Equipped Kitchen
▼ ▲ ▼ ▲ ▼ ▲ ▼ ▲ ▲ ▼ ▲ ▼ ▲ ▼

To prepare the recipes in *Cody Coyote Cooks!*, you'll need to have the following equipment in your kitchen. If you don't have a particular utensil, check with an adult to see if something could be substituted.

baking pans and dishes
baking sheets
biscuit cutter (3-inch size)
butter knives
can opener
diamond-shaped cookie cutters
grater
hot pads
ice cream scoop
measuring cups, liquid and dry
measuring spoons
microwave-safe plates
mixing bowls
pastry brush
pie plate (8- or 9-inch)
pitcher
pizza cutter
rolling pin
saucepans, medium and large
sharp knives, sized for smaller hands
spatula
spoons, large, metal and wooden
tongs

Cody Coyote and the Tall Texas Tale

The moon had risen three times since Cody Coyote had eaten, and he was hungry! The vast Texas range was dotted with cactus and tumbleweeds, two things that any respectable coyote would not eat. "AHOOOOOOO," Cody howled, and waited for a reply. He heard nothing. "AHOOOOOOO, AHOOOOOOO." Again silence. "If I could only find some other coyotes, I know they would have something great to eat," he said to himself.

As Cody walked down the road, along came an armadillo. "Howdy, Mr. Coyote. Where are you headin'? Mind if I join you?" Now you see, Cody had never tasted an armadillo before. His hungry brain began to scheme. "That varmint's not the most attractive-looking animal. But hey, if I could get through that armor stuff, he could make a tasty meal!"

Armadillo began ambling next to Cody. "My name is Cody Coyote, and I'd like to challenge you to a race. I heard you're the fastest in the desert." Cody knew he was a great trickster. Certainly he could outrun this weird-looking animal, and then when Armadillo tired, he would capture him and eat him for dinner.

"That sounds like a heap of fun, Cody. I just hope I don't whup you too badly," said Armadillo cheerfully.

"Ready, set, go!" Cody yelled. It was now or never. Cody

leaped to grab Armadillo, but he tucked his body into a round ball and rolled away, down the road to safety.

"Shucks!" said Cody. "He probably would have been too tough anyway. Guess I'll have to find something else for dinner."

Cody was now not only hungry, but cranky and tired, too. He called out to his brothers again. Still no answer.

The sun finally went down, and the moon had taken its place in the sky. Cody let out an "AHOOOOOOO." This time he heard a howl back. He danced a little jig in the sand, and with all of the strength he could muster, Cody ran toward the howls. But even as he ran, he thought, "These howls don't sound like the ones I usually hear," but these were Texas Coyotes, so maybe their songs were different from Cody's New Mexican friends.

"AHOOOOOOO," Cody wailed. "Why aren't they calling back to me?" When he stepped from behind some bushes, Cody yelped "YIKES" and quickly covered his mouth. Humans were sitting around a campfire serenading the night. "They're trying to sound like coyotes! For shame!" Cody was all set to turn around and leave in disgust, but he got a whiff of some wonderful smells from the campfire—smoky beef jerky, juicy sausage, hot potatoes, flaky biscuits...It was all more than he could bear. He had to get some of that food! He circled the cowboy camp and came up with a wonderful tricky plan. Slowly, quietly, he crawled over to the humans' horses, then jumped up and let out a howl. "AHOOOOOOO!" The startled horses reared up and whinnied. They yanked at their ropes until they were free, then dashed off into the darkness with the cowboys chasing.

Cody ran down to the dying fire and grabbed some food—and managed to burn his nose on the coals. "Ouch!" he yipped and scampered off with his meal. He licked his stinging nose, devoured all the food in six big gulps, and then fell soundly asleep under a bush.

The next morning, Cody awoke to see a red bandanna hanging on a branch. "Holy smokes!" said Cody to himself. "One of the cowboys left a beautiful red scarf for me." He put the bandanna on and went over to a stream to gaze proudly at his reflection. The bandanna looked great, but his once perfectly pink nose had turned black! And that is why, to this very day, whenever you see a coyote, his nose is always black.

Cowboy Recipes

Tall Texas Tea

Beginner   Beverage; makes 4 servings

Better than sarsaparilla (a soft drink flavored with dried roots), this tall drink is great after riding the dusty trails!

You will need:
1 pitcher
1 large mixing spoon
Measuring cup

3 cups decaffeinated iced tea (try the Sun Tea recipe, following)
$^1/_2$ cup orange juice
$^1/_2$ cup lemonade

What to do:
1. In a large pitcher, mix together iced tea, orange juice, and lemonade.
2. Refrigerate. Pour into glasses and serve.

 Coyote caution: *Be sure to refrigerate any drink immediately that has fruit juice in it.*

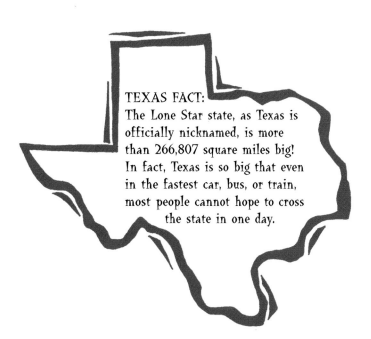

TEXAS FACT:
The Lone Star state, as Texas is officially nicknamed, is more than 266,807 square miles big! In fact, Texas is so big that even in the fastest car, bus, or train, most people cannot hope to cross the state in one day.

Sun Tea

Beginner   BEVERAGE; MAKES 4 CUPS

This tea will be ready lickity-split! It takes about 20 minutes to brew 4 cups.

You will need:

1 quart glass container with a lid

3 bags of your favorite decaffeinated tea
3 cups water

What to do:

1. Place the tea bags and the water in a glass jar, placing the lid on tightly.
2. Put the jar in the sun until the water turns dark.

 Coyote caution: *Never put artificial sweetener in the tea before you put it in the sun, as it will ferment!*

TEXAS FACT:
On December 29, 1845, Texas became the twenty-eighth state.

Purple Cow

Beginner

Not even Cody Coyote has visited a real purple cow on his adventures (although he's been seen sneaking a sip or two of one when no one was looking).

You will need:
4 tall glasses
1 ice cream scoop
Measuring cup

4 cups grape juice
2 cups club soda or lemon-lime soda
4 scoops vanilla ice cream

What to do:
1. Pour 1 cup of the grape juice and $^1/_2$ cup of the soda into each glass.
2. Place one scoop of ice cream in the grape juice mixture and serve.

Coyote hint: *Be sure to rinse the ice cream scoop as soon as you're done with it. Place the ice cream in the glass carefully and slowly so that it doesn't splatter and make a mess.*

Beginner

Bedrolls
(Cream Cheese and Jelly)

FINGER FOOD; MAKES 4 SERVINGS

"Bedroll" is the cowboy word for sleeping bag. These round sandwiches roll up so that they can be carried as easily as a cowboy bed! You may even want to make your own tortillas. Try the recipe on p. 34. When you make these bedrolls, we guarantee no crust and lots of fun.

You will need:

1 butter knife
Tablespoon

4 flour tortillas
4 tablespoons cream cheese
4 tablespoons jelly or jam

What to do:

1. Spread 1 tablespoon cream cheese and 1 tablespoon jelly on one side of each tortilla.
2. Beginning at one end, roll the tortillas up as tightly as possible.
3. Serve the bedrolls as you would a sandwich, or cut them into 1-inch spirals for a snack.

Coyote caution: *Be sure to roll these tightly. If they don't stay rolled, secure them with toothpicks. Always remove toothpicks before serving.*

Bedrolls
(Ham and Cheese)

Beginner

FINGER FOOD; MAKES 4 SERVINGS

Bedrolls are a perfect take-along food for the busy cowboy; they can be eaten on horseback!

You will need:

Microwave-safe plate (if you want warm bedrolls)
1 butter knife
Hot pads

4 flour tortillas
8 thin slices boiled ham
8 thin slices American cheese
Mustard or mayonnaise (optional)

What to do:

1. Place 1 tortilla on a plate.
2. Place 2 slices ham and 2 slices cheese on the tortilla. If you wish, spread a bit of mustard or mayonnaise with a knife.
3. Beginning at one end, roll the tortilla up tightly.
4. Repeat for each tortilla.
5. You can serve the bedrolls at room temperature, or you can warm them in a microwave oven. To warm them, place the bedrolls on a microwave-safe plate. Microwave the bedrolls on high 30 seconds, turn the plate a half turn and microwave another 20 seconds or until the cheese melts.

Coyote caution: *Be sure to microwave the bedrolls on a microwave safe-plate, in case the cheese melts and runs outside of the tortilla. Always use a hot pad when removing plates from the microwave, because they might get hot!*

Dried Hide

Intermediate

Dried hide is the perfect food to take along on a hike or bike ride.

You will need:

1 large baking sheet
Aluminum foil
1 large sealable plastic bag
Paper towels
Measuring cup
Measuring spoons
Hot pads

TEXAS FACT:
Texas was named for the Native American word *tejas*, meaning "friend." The Texas state motto is "Friendship."

$^1/_3$ cup soy sauce
$^2/_3$ cup water
$^1/_2$ teaspoon liquid smoke
$^1/_4$ teaspoon garlic powder
$^1/_4$ teaspoon black pepper
1 pound beef roast, sliced thinly by the butcher or an adult coyote (flank steak or eye of round work best)

What to do:

1. Put the soy sauce, water, liquid smoke, garlic powder, and pepper in the plastic bag and mix.
2. Place the sliced meat in the marinade and seal the bag. Let the meat marinate in the refrigerator for 1 hour or longer.
3. Remove the meat strips from the marinade and drain on paper towels. Lay the meat strips on a foil-lined baking sheet.
4. Place the pan in a warm oven, about 150°, for 6 to 8 hours, or until the meat is completely dried and breaks when you bend it. Turn the meat strips every 2 hours so that the meat will dry evenly. Once done, the meat should have a leathery texture.

5. Store in an airtight container, such as a sealable plastic bag, in the refrigerator for up to 2 to 3 weeks.

 Coyote caution: *Always have the butcher slice the meat for jerky, as it must be very thin and uniformly sliced to make successful Dried Hide.*

 ## Spurs and Such, Munchin' Stuff

Beginner   FINGER FOOD; MAKES 3 CUPS

A yummy mix of sorts, this snack will power you up for a great day, whether you're riding horses or chasing cows!

You will need:
    1 large mixing bowl
    1 large spoon
    Measuring cup

    $1/2$ cup cashews
    $1/2$ cup pecans
    $1/2$ cup sunflower seeds
    $1/2$ cup dried apples
    $1/2$ cup dried apricots
    $1/2$ cup raisins

What to do:
1. Place nuts, dried fruits, and raisins in a large mixing bowl; stir to mix thoroughly.
2. Store in airtight, sealable plastic bags and in a dry place.

 Coyote hint: *Vary your munchin' stuff by adding or substituting chocolate chips, different dried fruits, different nuts, and jelly beans or other small candies.*

Sidewinder Sausages

Intermediate

Try Sidewinder Sausages on the grill or cooked the cowboy way over a campfire, but look out for real sidewinder snakes which travel sideways through the sandy desert.

You will need:

    1 pastry brush
    1 large baking dish
    Measuring cup
    Hot pads
    Tongs

    1 pound Polish sausage, kielbasa,
        or summer sausage
    1 cup barbecue sauce

> **TEXAS FACT:**
> The mockingbird, the pecan tree, and the bluebonnet are the state bird, tree, and flower of Texas.

What to do:

1. Preheat the oven to 350°.
2. Place the sausages in one layer in a baking dish and brush some of the barbecue sauce onto them with the pastry brush.
3. Put the baking dish into the oven and bake until the sausages are heated through, about 30 minutes.
4. Using hot pads, carefully remove the baking dish from the oven. Brush the sausages with additional sauce and serve. An adult coyote should help use tongs to remove the sausages from the baking dish.

Coyote caution: *Be sure to use precooked sausage when making this recipe. Before removing the hot dish from the oven, have a place ready that can take the heat; don't put it directly on a Formica counter.*

Get Along Little Doggies

Beginner   MAIN DISH; MAKES 4 SERVINGS

Hot dogs and beans are a cowboy favorite. These dogs won't bark and they don't bite back!

You will need:
    1 large saucepan
    1 large mixing spoon
    Can opener
    1 butter knife
    Hot pads

    1 can (15 ounces) pork
        and beans
    4 hot dogs

> **TEXAS FACT:**
> When a cowboy calls out "get along little dogies," he is actually leading orphan calves, not dogs, back to the herd.

What to do:
1. Open the can of pork and beans and pour them into the saucepan.
2. Cut hot dogs into 1-inch slices and add the hot dogs to the beans. Stir to combine.
3. Cook and stir over medium heat until mixture is hot and the hot dogs are heated through.

 Coyote caution: *Be sure to stir the mixture so that it heats evenly and doesn't burn. Be careful when cutting up the hot dogs; it is best to ask an adult for help with this.*

MacChili

MAIN DISH; MAKES 4 SERVINGS

This chili and macaroni dish is perfect for a bit of kitchen creativity. Try different kinds of pasta; macaroni, shells, wagon wheels, and spirals work great! As the cowboys say, when you've been on the range a long time, this dish is definitely "better than nuttin."

You will need:

    1 large saucepan
    1 large mixing spoon
    Can opener
    Grater
    Measuring cup
    Hot pads

    2 cans (15 ounces each) chili
        with meat, no beans
    2 cups cooked macaroni (start with 1 cup
        dried macaroni)
    $1/2$ cup grated Cheddar cheese

> TEXAS FACT:
> You might have heard the phrase "Remember the Alamo." That saying came from one of Texas' most famous battles, which was fought at the Alamo, an old Spanish mission, in 1836.

What to do:

1. Open cans of chili and pour into a large saucepan.
2. Heat and stir over medium heat until chili is heated through.
3. Add cooked macaroni and stir until mixed and macaroni is heated.
4. Serve with grated cheese on top.

Coyote caution: *Be sure to stir the mixture while it is heating so that it won't burn.*

Butter in a Bottle

Beginner

Remember how long it took Cody Coyote to find something good to eat? Be patient; this recipe takes a little while too, but it's worth it!

You will need:
    1 large jar with tight-fitting lid
    1 marble
    Measuring cup
    Teaspoon

    $^{1}/_{3}$ cup whipping cream, extra heavy if you can find it
    $^{1}/_{4}$ teaspoon salt

What to do:
1. Pour the whipping cream into a jar, put in the marble, and tighten the lid.
2. Shake, shake, shake until a solid starts to form; keep shaking until butter is formed, about 10 to 15 minutes.
3. Pour off the buttermilk and remove the marble.
4. Stir the salt into the butter to taste.

 Coyote caution: *Be sure the lid is on very tight so the mixture doesn't spill.*

Branding Iron Biscuits

Beginner

Every cattle ranch has its own special brand; sometimes it is the initials of the owner's name, a symbol such as a star, or a circle with letters in it. What would your brand look like?

You will need:
  1 baking sheet
  1 small bowl
  1 fork
  1 very small paintbrush, new and unused
  1 very small spatula
  Hot pads

  1 package refrigerator biscuits
  1 egg

What to do:
1. Preheat the oven to 400°.
2. Place each biscuit on the baking sheet.

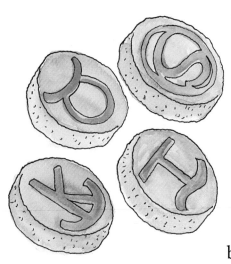

3. Separate the egg yolk from the egg white, place the egg yolk in a small bowl, and stir until smooth. (Save the egg white for another use, or throw it away.) Dip paintbrush in yolk and draw your brand on each biscuit.
4. Bake the biscuits in the oven for 10 to 12 minutes, or until they are browned. Using hot pads, remove the baking sheet from the oven and let the

biscuits cool for a few minutes before serving. Use a spatula to remove the biscuits from the baking sheet.

 Coyote caution: *Be careful when opening the biscuit package. Sometimes it pops from the pressure it is packed with.*

 ## Campfire Fries

Side dish or finger food; makes 4 servings

Intermediate

These fries work great in the coals of a barbecue grill or, of course, on a campfire. Wrap them in two layers of foil if you're going to prepare them this way.

You will need:
> 2 sheets of heavy-duty aluminum
>   foil, each about 15 inches long
> Potato peeler (optional)
> 1 sharp knife
> Grater
> Nonstick vegetable cooking
>   spray
> 1 baking sheet
> Measuring cup
> Hot pads

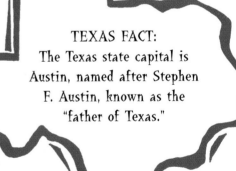

TEXAS FACT:
The Texas state capital is Austin, named after Stephen F. Austin, known as the "father of Texas."

> 2 large potatoes, cut into french fry strips about
> $1/4$ inch thick (if you prefer fries without the peel,
>   peel the potatoes before you cut them into strips)
> $1/2$ cup grated Colby or Cheddar cheese
> Seasoned salt

What to do:

1. Preheat the oven to 350°.
2. Place one sheet of the foil on a baking sheet and lightly spray the foil with the vegetable cooking spray.
3. Put the potato strips onto the foil, leaving 3 inches of border around the edge of the foil, then cover with the cheese and sprinkle seasoned salt lightly over the cheese.
4. Place the second sheet of foil over the potato mixture.
5. Double-fold all edges so you have a foil packet.
6. Place the baking sheet with the packet into the oven and bake for 30 minutes. Using hot pads, remove the baking sheet from the oven. Let the packet cool for 10 minutes before serving.

 Coyote caution: *Whenever you cut a potato, first cut it in half and then place it flat side down so the potato can't roll. Ask an adult coyote for help with the first cut.*

Let the foil cool a little before removing the fries. Have an adult coyote remove the top foil from the packet.

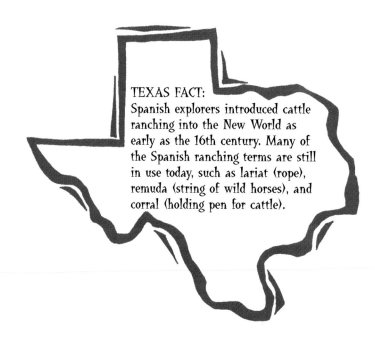

TEXAS FACT:
Spanish explorers introduced cattle ranching into the New World as early as the 16th century. Many of the Spanish ranching terms are still in use today, such as lariat (rope), remuda (string of wild horses), and corral (holding pen for cattle).

Howlin' Coyote Toast

Beginner

This grub is so good you'll howl at the moon for more!

You will need:
   1 baking pan
   Serrated knife or bread knife
   Grater
   Measuring cup
   Hot pads
   Tongs

   1 long loaf French or sourdough bread
   1 cup grated cheese, Colby and Monterey Jack combined

What to do:
1. Preheat the oven to 400°.
2. Cut the bread into 4-inch slices and then cut each section in half lengthwise.
3. Sprinkle the top of each bread slice with some of the grated cheese.
4. Place the bread slices on the baking sheet and place the baking sheet into the oven. Bake for 10 minutes, or until the cheese melts. Using hot pads, remove the baking sheet from the oven and let the bread cool for a few minutes before serving. Use tongs to remove the bread from the baking sheet.

 Coyote caution: *Use a special bread knife to cut French bread; it is safer and will be easier to cut with. Cut bread with a sawing motion, and always have an adult coyote help when slicing.*

Wild Filly Frito Pie

MAIN DISH; MAKES 4 TO 6 SERVINGS

Intermediate

This is every cowboy's favorite! If you're feeling adventurous, you may want to put a little hot sauce or sour cream on top.

You will need:

1 pie pan, 9 or 10 inches across
1 large, heavy, sealable plastic freezer bag
1 rolling pin
Grater
1 frying pan
1 large mixing spoon
Measuring cup
Hot pads
Wire rack
1 pie server or spatula

3 cups tortilla chips or Fritos®
1 pound extra-lean ground beef
1 can (8 ounces) tomato sauce
$^1/_2$ cup cooked corn
$^1/_2$ teaspoon chili powder (optional)
1 cup grated Colby cheese

What to do:

1. Preheat the oven to 350°.
2. Place tortilla chips or Fritos® in a large plastic bag. Pound them into crumbs with a rolling pin. Measure the crumbs; you should have $1^1/_2$ cups.
3. Brown the ground beef in a frying pan over medium-high heat, cooking it until it is no longer pink and is nicely

browned. Use a spoon to stir the meat and to break it up into chunks as it cooks. Stir in tomato sauce, cooked corn, and chili powder.

4. Put 1 cup of the crushed chips in the bottom of the pie pan and spread them evenly to cover the bottom. Carefully spoon the hamburger mixture on top of the crushed chips. Sprinkle the grated cheese over the hamburger mixture and then sprinkle remaining $1/2$ cup of crushed chips over the cheese.

5. Place the pie in the oven and bake for 15 to 20 minutes, or until the cheese is melted and the pie is heated through. Using hot pads, remove the pie from the oven and place it on a wire rack to cool for 5 minutes. Slice into wedges and serve, using a pie server or spatula.

 Coyote caution: *Let the pie cool on a wire rack for 5 minutes before cutting it into wedges and serving. You can freeze any leftovers.*

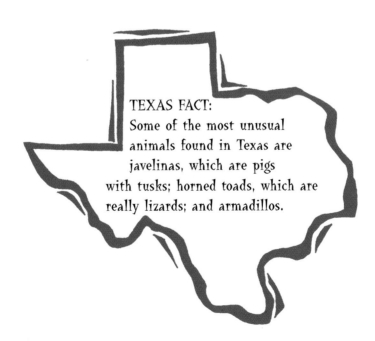

TEXAS FACT:
Some of the most unusual animals found in Texas are javelinas, which are pigs with tusks; horned toads, which are really lizards; and armadillos.

Rocky Mountain Mud Pie

Intermediate

DESSERT; MAKES 4 LARGE SERVINGS OR 8 SMALL SERVINGS

We guarantee this to be the best mud in the West!

You will need:

1 baking sheet
1 mixing bowl
1 mixing spoon
Measuring cups
Hot pads
Wire rack
Pie server or spatula

1 package brownie mix, standard size 19.8 to 23.5 ounces,
    plus oil, eggs, and water as directed on the package
$1/2$ cup prechopped walnuts
1 prepared pie crust in a pie tin (you can purchase these in
    the frozen food section)
Whipped cream (optional)

What to do:

1. Preheat the oven to 350°.
2. Prepare the brownie mix in a mixing bowl according to package directions, adding oil, eggs, and water as directed. Leave the brownie batter in the bowl; set aside.
3. Place the pie tin with the prepared pie crust on a baking sheet. Pour in the nuts to cover the bottom of the pie shell.
4. Spoon 2 cups of the brownie batter over the nuts in the pie shell. Smooth the top of the mixture so it is level.
5. Place the mud pie, still on the baking sheet, in the oven to bake for 30 minutes. Using hot pads, remove the pie from the oven and let it cool on a wire rack. Slice into wedges and serve,

using a pie server or spatula. (Top each serving with a dollop of whipped cream if you like.)

 Coyote caution: *Be sure to bake the pie on top of a baking sheet in case the mixture spills over out of the pie shell.*

 Coyote hint: *Make regular brownies with any leftover brownie mix; they won't go to waste!*

 Cow Chip Cookies

DESSERT; MAKES 4 DOZEN

Intermediate

Here are some cookies that don't need baking. You won't find any of these cow chips along the trail!

You will need:
1 baking sheet
Waxed paper
1 large saucepan
1 large mixing spoon
Measuring spoons
Measuring cups
Hot pads

TEXAS FACT:
Speaking of cows, Texas is the home of longhorn cattle, so named because of the enormous length of their horns—sometimes they measure more than 12 feet from tip to tip!

2 cups sugar
5 tablespoons unsweetened cocoa
$1/2$ cup milk
$1/2$ cup butter (1 stick)
$1/2$ cup chunky peanut butter
1 teaspoon vanilla extract
3 cups quick-cooking oats
$1/2$ cup prechopped nuts

What to do:
1. Cover baking sheet with waxed paper and set aside.
2. Combine sugar and cocoa in a large saucepan. Stir in milk, butter, and peanut butter. Cook and stir over medium heat until butter melts and mixture is combined, about 5 to 10 minutes.
3. Turn the heat off, stir in the vanilla extract, oats, and nuts, and mix thoroughly.
4. Take a teaspoon and scoop out a spoonful of the mixture; drop the spoonful onto the waxed paper–covered baking sheet. Repeat with the rest of the mixture. Place in the refrigerator until the cookies are cooled and set. Store cookies in an airtight container.

 Coyote caution: *Be sure to remove the mixture of milk, butter, and peanut butter from the heat before you add the oats and nuts; this will prevent the mixture from burning and will allow the mixture to start cooling so you can safely spoon it out.*

 Armadillo Rolls

Beginner   DESSERT; MAKES $^1/_2$ POUND CANDY

Many armadillos are found in Texas, where they really do roll up into a ball when they get scared!

You will need:
    1 mixing bowl
    1 large mixing spoon
    1 plate
    Measuring cup

1 cup sunflower seeds or pine nuts or prechopped nuts
1 cup peanut butter
1 cup corn syrup
1 cup powdered sugar

What to do:
1. Place seeds or chopped nuts on a plate and set aside.
2. In a mixing bowl, mix together the peanut butter, corn syrup, and powdered sugar until well blended.
3. Roll the mixture into little balls, and roll these balls in the nuts until the balls are completely covered.

 Coyote hint: *If the mixture is too sticky, sprinkle powdered sugar on your hands to keep the mixture from sticking to you.*

 # Bandanna Backpack

Beginner   CRAFT; MAKES 1 BANDANNA BACKPACK

Hook your bandanna backpack onto your saddle and hit the trail!

You will need:
    1 large bandanna or scarf

    A snack or something you need to carry

What to do:
1. Lay the bandanna flat.
2. Place the snack or whatever in the center of the bandanna.
3. Take two opposite corners and bring them to the center; tie a knot in the ends. Then take the remaining ends and tie them into a knot. (This will form a pouch.)
4. You can carry your bandanna backpack or hook it onto something, like your bike or a sturdy stick.

Cody Coyote and the Siesta Fiesta

"If only I could fly like the Raven, I could see the path ahead of me," Cody said. He envied other animals, and dreamt longingly of doing everything that they could do—but, he usually got into trouble trying to imitate his neighbors, and that's where our story begins.

As much as he wanted to fly, Cody also wanted to eat. He knew that in the Land of Enchantment—that's New Mexico—it was the season of harvest fiestas. There would be an abundance of corn, chiles, and yummy desserts. Cody could almost taste the foods of the feast day—and he wanted to take the quickest route. Watching a flock of ravens in graceful flight, Cody said with a sigh, "Oh how I wish I had beautiful, black shiny wings."

"Helloooo, Ravens," Cody called. "Would you let me know where the party is? It's *muy importante!*"

The ravens circled around to Cody. "Sure," they called out, "follow us!" As the ravens began to fly, Cody ran faster and faster. But no matter how hard he tried, he couldn't run fast enough to keep up. "Come on guys, teach me to fly," begged Cody. "Pretty please, with birdseed on top!" The birds each plucked one feather and gave it to Cody, who quickly built two large wings which he attached to his front legs. He was ready for his test flight.

Cody flapped the new wings as fast as he could, and soon he was actually flying! But just as he was about as high as the other

birds, one by one, then six by six, the feathers fell to the ground. And so did Cody. Luckily, right onto a tumbleweed.

"Sorry, Cody, coyotes were just not meant to fly," the ravens yelled from high above.

But Cody was not about to give up—not if food was involved. Fortunately, he had managed to fly far enough to hear the faint sounds of music over the next hill.

Sounds of the celebration led Cody down a long trail to a New Mexican village. As he got closer, he could see the dancing and the colorful costumes, hear laughter and singing, and best of all, smell glorious food—chiles, chocolate, and corn tortillas were everywhere.

Cody cautiously approached the celebration—then stopped in horror. A coyote was hanging from a tree as children laughed and hit him with sticks!

"I must save Brother Coyote!" cried Cody as he headed for the awful scene. But before he could help, the coyote exploded, and candy rained down over the children. Brother Coyote was really a *piñata*.

Although Cody was angry for being tricked (He liked tricking others, not the other way around), he was much more interested in getting his paws on some food. But each time he approached the banquet, the humans would shoo him away, and then go back to dancing around a large velvet hat called a *sombrero*.

"Alrighty, let them be that way," muttered Cody. "There is certainly more than one way to snatch a feast-day snack or two! If only they'd take a rest for a while, maybe a little *siesta*." As he paced around thinking of a plan, he tripped over a scrawny bush. "Hey! Watch where you're..." But then he realized that the bush was his answer: it was really a little piñon tree full of magic nuts! As all coyotes know, anyone who ate a magic nut would fall into a deep sleep.

Very quietly and slowly, Cody crept over to the place where the villagers stored the *champurro* drink that was made especially for the fiesta. "One for you, and one for you, and..." Cody plopped a nut into each drink. And then he waited. One by one, the villagers drank and one by one each fell soundly asleep. When the last villager was snoring loudly, Cody ran over to the banquet table and ate everything he possibly could: flour tortillas, bean burritos, empanadas, and feast day cookies.

When his tummy was full, Cody knew it was time to leave before the villagers woke up—but first he wanted a souvenir. He picked up the *sombrero* and slapped it on his head. As he scampered off, Coyote chuckled, "This was indeed a fine *siesta* fiesta!"

New Mexican Recipes

New Mexican Moo Juice

Beginner

BEVERAGE; MAKES 4 SERVINGS

In New Mexico, hot chocolate is called *champurro.* With this awesome drink, you get to have candy bars in a cup!

You will need:
1 large saucepan
1 large mixing spoon
Measuring cup
Measuring spoons
Mugs or coffee cups

2 small milk chocolate candy bars
     (1.55-ounce size)
1 1/2 cups milk
1/2 cup half-and-half (light cream)
1 teaspoon vanilla extract
Whipped cream (optional)

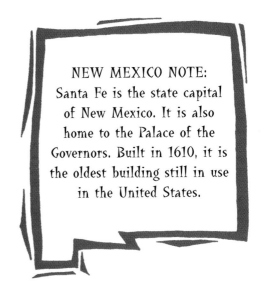

NEW MEXICO NOTE:
Santa Fe is the state capital of New Mexico. It is also home to the Palace of the Governors. Built in 1610, it is the oldest building still in use in the United States.

What to do:
1. Break the chocolate bars into very small pieces.
2. Combine the milk, half-and-half, chocolate, and vanilla extract in a large saucepan.
3. Heat over medium heat until chocolate melts and mixture is warmed through. Do not boil.
4. Serve in mugs or coffee cups; top with whipped cream, if desired.

 Coyote caution: *Have an adult coyote pour the hot chocolate into the mugs. Always serve hot chocolate in heatproof mugs or coffee cups, never in glasses.*

Homemade Corn Tortillas

Intermediate

Tortillas are prepared and eaten at almost every traditional feast day party. They're great fun to make; however, a big coyote (an adult) must help you cook them. Do not attempt this recipe without first asking an adult for help!

You will need:
> 1 large mixing bowl
> 1 fork
> Measuring spoons
> Measuring cups
> 1 rolling pin or tortilla press
> Waxed paper
> 1 large frying pan
> Nonstick vegetable cooking spray
> Tongs
> Paper towels

> 2 cups corn flour (*masa harina*)
> $^3/_4$ teaspoon salt
> 1 cup water (a little more, if necessary)
> $^1/_4$ cup all-purpose flour

What to do:
1. In a large mixing bowl, mix together the corn flour and salt with a fork.
2. Add the water, a little at a time, while mixing with the fork until the mixture forms a dough.
3. Knead the dough by pressing and folding it with your hands for a minute. If it seems dry and won't hold together, add a little more water.

4. Divide the dough into 12 balls.

5. Sprinkle 2 sheets of waxed paper lightly with some of the flour and place one ball of dough between the 2 sheets. Roll out with a rolling pin until the tortilla is as thin as possible. You may also use a tortilla press or pat the dough flat with your hands.

6. Spray the bottom of a frying pan with nonstick vegetable cooking spray. Heat the pan over high heat, and place 1 tortilla at a time in the pan. When the tortilla is lightly browned on one side (check it often!), turn it over with the tongs and cook the other side. The whole process should take less than a minute. The tortilla should still be soft, not crisp. Remove the tortilla from the pan with the tongs and place on paper towels. Repeat this step for each tortilla. (Be sure to spray the pan before cooking each one.) Use the tortillas for tacos, nachos, and other New Mexican recipes.

 Coyote hint: *If the tortilla dough sticks to the waxed paper, sprinkle it with more flour.*

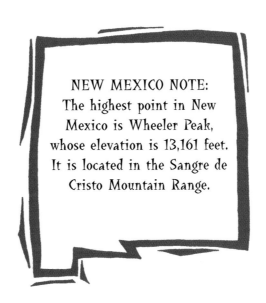

NEW MEXICO NOTE:
The highest point in New Mexico is Wheeler Peak, whose elevation is 13,161 feet. It is located in the Sangre de Cristo Mountain Range.

Homemade Flour Tortillas

Intermediate

Use flour tortillas as you would bread; that's the New Mexican tradition. Have an adult coyote help you cook these.

You will need:
    1 large mixing bowl
    1 fork
    Measuring spoons
    Measuring cups
    Waxed paper
    1 rolling pin or tortilla press
    1 large frying pan
    Nonstick vegetable cooking spray
    Tongs
    Paper towels

    $^1/_4$ teaspoon baking powder
    $^1/_2$ teaspoon salt
    1 cup flour, plus more for sprinkling on the waxed paper
    1 tablespoon lard or shortening
    1 tablespoon water (more or less)

What to do:
1. In a large bowl mix together the baking powder, salt, and flour with a fork.
2. Add the lard or shortening in little pieces the size of peas. With a fork, blend the lard into the flour.
3. Slowly add the water a little at a time until the mixture forms a smooth dough.
4. Divide the dough into 6 balls.

5. Sprinkle 2 sheets of waxed paper lightly with flour. Place 1 ball of dough between the 2 sheets. With a rolling pin, roll out the dough until the tortilla is as thin as possible. You can also use a tortilla press or pat them flat with your hands.

6. Spray the bottom of a frying pan with nonstick vegetable cooking spray. Heat the pan over high heat, and place one tortilla at a time in the pan. When the tortilla is lightly browned on one side (check it often!), turn it over with the tongs and cook the other side. The whole process should take less than a minute. The tortilla should still be soft, not crisp. Remove the tortilla from the pan with the tongs and place on paper towels. Repeat this step for each tortilla. (Be sure to spray the pan before cooking each one.) Flour tortillas are used in many New Mexican recipes, or you can just warm them in a frying pan and eat them with butter.

 Coyote caution: *Be sure to watch the tortillas carefully so that they do not burn.*

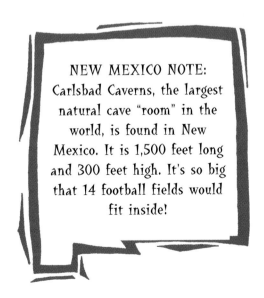

NEW MEXICO NOTE:
Carlsbad Caverns, the largest natural cave "room" in the world, is found in New Mexico. It is 1,500 feet long and 300 feet high. It's so big that 14 football fields would fit inside!

Bunch o' Muncho Nachos

Beginner

FINGER FOOD; MAKES 4 SERVINGS

These are the best munchable, crunchable snacks! For fun, why not add salsa, sliced olives, or cooked hamburger before microwaving. Better yet, top the nachos with sour cream, lettuce, chopped tomatoes, or guacamole before serving. Customize your nachos with what *you* like!

You will need:
>1 microwave-safe glass pie plate
>Grater
>Measuring cup
>Hot pads

>4 cups tortilla chips
>1 cup grated Cheddar cheese
>1 cup grated Monterey Jack cheese
>Jalapeño slices, if you're brave, or canned diced green chiles

What to do:
1. Layer the tortilla chips on the glass pie plate, and sprinkle the cheese over the top.
2. If you're brave, add a few jalapeño slices or some diced green chiles (these are not very hot), only as much as you want.
3. Microwave the nachos on high for 1 minute. Check to see if the cheese is melted. If it is, carefully remove the plate from the microwave, using hot pads, and serve. If the cheese isn't melted, microwave the nachos on high for 20 seconds at a time until the cheese is melted.

Coyote caution: *Always use hot pads to remove plates from the microwave, as sometimes plates can get hot.*

Advanced

Sizzlin' Sombreros

FINGER FOOD; MAKES 6 SOMBREROS

Empanadas are little dough pockets that look like tiny sombreros. Although these are filled with beef, there are many other possible fillings. Some are even filled with fruit or chocolate.

You will need:
1 baking sheet
3-inch biscuit cutter
Grater
1 frying pan
1 fork
Floured surface
Measuring cups
Tablespoon
Hot pads
Spatula

$1/2$ pound extra-lean ground beef
3 cups grated Cheddar cheese
1 cup taco sauce
2 prepared pie crusts

What to do:
1. Preheat the oven to 400°.
2. In a large frying pan, brown and crumble the ground beef, cooking the beef until it is no longer pink but has browned thoroughly.
3. Stir in the cheese and taco sauce, remove the frying pan from the heat, and set aside.
4. If you are using a purchased pie crust, lightly flour a large board or table and tip the crust out of its pie tin. Press it flat.

5. With a biscuit cutter, cut circles in the pie dough. Place a tablespoon of meat mixture in the center of half of the circles.

6. Cover each with a second circle of dough. Press the edges together to seal them. Use a fork if you have trouble getting the dough to stick together. Pull up the edge and pinch the dough together to make sombrero shape.

7. Place the sombreros on a baking sheet and bake for 12 to 14 minutes, or until they are golden brown. Using hot pads, remove the baking sheet from the oven and let the sombreros cool for a few minutes before serving. Use a spatula to remove them from the pan.

 Coyote hint: *Be sure the empanadas are completely sealed so the filling doesn't leak out.*

Burros

MAIN DISH; MAKES 4 SERVINGS

Intermediate

Burros, or bean burritos, are the original sandwich from Mexico, perfect to make and go! Try adding cooked ground beef, or cooked cubed chicken, to the bean mixture. It's great! To make your own flour tortillas, see page 34.

You will need:
1 baking sheet
Aluminum foil
Grater

Measuring cup
Tablespoon
Hot pads

4 large flour tortillas
1 can (16 ounces) refried beans
2 cups grated Cheddar cheese
4 tablespoons taco sauce

What to do:

1. Preheat the oven to 350°.
2. Place 1 tortilla on a sheet of aluminum foil.
3. Spread $^1/_4$ cup of refried beans in the center of the tortilla.
4. Top with $^1/_2$ cup cheese and 1 tablespoon taco sauce.
5. Fold both ends of the tortilla over the bean and cheese mixture, then roll the burrito up. Wrap the foil around the burrito. Place on a baking sheet. Repeat with other tortillas.
6. Bake for 20 minutes, or until heated through. Using hot pads, remove the baking sheet from the oven. Carefully remove the burros from the foil and eat.

 Coyote hint: *If the flour tortillas start breaking when you're trying to fold the burritos, simply warm them in the microwave for 10 seconds and they will be easier to work with. Or remove the tortillas from the refrigerator before you get started, and let them warm to room temperature.*

 Coyote caution: *Be sure never to put foil in the microwave.*

Hotter than You-Know-What Salsa

Intermediate

This special dip can be mighty hot. We suggest you start out with mild chiles; you'll like it a lot!

You will need:

    1 mixing bowl
    1 mixing fork
    Measuring cup
    1 serrated steak knife
    Tablespoon

    $1/3$ cup tomato purée
    1 small can (4 ounces) chopped
        green chiles
    1 cup stewed tomatoes, chopped
    1 tablespoon diced onion
        (optional)
    Chopped green chiles or jalapeños to taste (optional)

> **NEW MEXICO NOTE:**
> Speaking of chiles, the chile pepper is the official state vegetable—even though it is really a fruit! They say more chiles are eaten and grown in New Mexico than in any other state. (Fifty-three million tons are grown there each year, but a lot of them are shipped to chile lovers in other states.)

What to do:

1. Mix together the tomato purée, green chiles, stewed tomatoes, and onion in a large mixing bowl.
2. Serve with tortilla chips.
3. If you like hot salsa, add a few jalapeños slices.

Coyote caution: *Always buy chopped chiles or jalapeños in a can or bottle; never try to dice or handle chiles; the oil from them can burn if you handle them and then touch your eyes or any other sensitive part of your body.*

Holy Moly Guacamole

Intermediate

To make your own salsa to go with this green treat, see page 40.

You can even grow your own avocado plant. Simply save the seed, wash and dry it, and then place it in a small, narrow-necked vase so that the broad side of the seed is covered with water. Make sure the base end is covered with water at all times. Keep the seed out of direct sunlight and change the water frequently until the bottom of the seed splits and roots emerge. This should take two to six weeks. After it grows a little more, place it in a sunny window and enjoy!

You will need:

1 large mixing bowl
1 large mixing fork
Butter knife or serrated knife to peel avocados
Measuring cup
Tablespoon

2 large avocados
$^1/_2$ cup salsa
2 tablespoons lemon juice

What to do:

1. Peel the avocados and remove the seeds. Break the avocados into small chunks. Place the chunks in a mixing bowl.
2. Stir in the salsa and lemon juice.
3. Serve with tortilla chips.

Coyote hint: *Always serve guacamole right after you have made it. If you need to keep it in the refrigerator, sprinkle additional lemon juice over the top of the dip to keep it from discoloring.*

Intermediate

Whole Lotta Tostada Salad

MAIN DISH; MAKES 4 SERVINGS

A great recipe like this could even tempt a coyote to eat his vegetables! To make your own salsa, see page 40.

You will need:

    4 serving plates or large salad bowls
    1 serrated steak knife
    Grater
    Measuring cup

    48 tortilla chips
    4 cups finely sliced and diced iceberg
        lettuce
    2 cups diced cooked chicken
    1 cup salsa
    1 cup grated Cheddar cheese
    $^1/_2$ cup sour cream

> NEW MEXICO NOTE: Nicknamed the Land of Enchantment, New Mexico became the forty-seventh state on January 6, 1912.

What to do:

1. Place 12 tortilla chips on each serving plate or in each salad bowl.
2. On top of the chips, layer one fourth of the lettuce, chicken, salsa, and cheese.
3. Top with a spoonful or dollop of sour cream in the center of each salad.

Coyote caution: *Assemble the salad just before serving so the tortilla chips don't get soggy.*

Zigzag Jicama

Beginner

Also known as the Mexican turnip, jicama is a great after-school snack. It tastes yummy dipped in salsa or on the Whole Lotta Tostada Salad.

You will need:
   1 large mixing bowl
   1 sharp knife
   Measuring cup

   2 cups peeled, sliced jicama ($^1\!/_2$-inch slices)
   $^1\!/_2$ cup lime juice

What to do:
1. Place the jicama in a large mixing bowl.
2. Pour lime juice over the jicama and toss to cover all slices.
3. Let the jicama marinate for 10 minutes. Remove the jicama from the lime juice and enjoy.

 Coyote caution: *Jicama has a very tough skin; always have an adult coyote peel and slice the jicama.*

Remind the big coyote to cut the jicama in half and place it cut side down on the cutting board so the jicama won't slip. The slices should be the size of french fries.

Chihuahua Cheese Crisps

Intermediate

FINGER FOOD; MAKES 4 SERVINGS

Did you know that not all pizza is Italian? New Mexican pizzas are great snacks and the perfect fiesta food.

You will need:

    1 baking sheet
    Grater
    1 sharp knife or pizza cutter
    Hot pads
    1 spatula
    Nonstick vegetable cooking spray

    4 flour tortillas
    2 cups grated Cheddar cheese
    Toppings of your choice: sliced black
        olives, chopped tomatoes, sliced mushrooms, and so on

NEW MEXICO NOTE:
New Mexico's state tree is the piñon, the state bird is the roadrunner, and the state flower is the yucca.

What to do:

1. Preheat the oven to 400°.
2. Place tortillas on a baking sheet and spray lightly with non-stick vegetable cooking spray.
3. Bake in oven for 5 minutes, or until tortillas get crispy (if not crispy, bake for another 2 minutes).
4. Using hot pads, remove the baking sheet from the oven and sprinkle each tortilla with cheese and the toppings of your choice.
5. Return sheet to oven and bake for another 5 minutes, or until cheese melts.
6. Using hot pads, remove the baking sheet from the oven and let the crisps cool for a minute or two. Using a spatula, remove the crisps to plates, cut into wedges, and serve.

Coyote caution: *Use hot pads to remove the baking sheet and be careful when adding toppings, as the baking sheet will be hot.*

 Peppy Pepitas

Beginner

FINGER FOOD; MAKES 1 CUP

These roasted pumpkin seeds are an authentic snack from Mexico.

You will need:
Strainer or colander
1 large baking sheet
Measuring cup
Measuring spoons
Hot pads
1 spatula
1 small paper bag

1 cup fresh pumpkin seeds
1 teaspoon vegetable oil
About ½ teaspoon salt

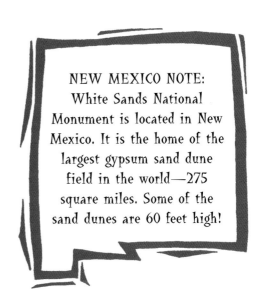

NEW MEXICO NOTE:
White Sands National Monument is located in New Mexico. It is the home of the largest gypsum sand dune field in the world—275 square miles. Some of the sand dunes are 60 feet high!

What to do:
1. Preheat the oven to 300°.
2. Place the pumpkin seeds in a strainer and rinse until clean. Be sure to remove any pulp left from the pumpkin.
3. Sprinkle the seeds onto the baking sheet and drizzle the oil over the seeds.
4. Place the baking sheet in the oven and bake for 15 to 20 minutes, or until the seeds are lightly browned.
5. Using hot pads, remove the baking sheet from the oven and let the seeds cool for a few minutes; then use a spatula to remove the seeds from the baking sheet and place them in a paper bag. Add salt and shake. Store the seeds in a sealable plastic bag.

Feast Day Cookies

DESSERT; MAKES 3 DOZEN COOKIES

Intermediate

These cookies are traditionally served at *fiestas* and also at weddings in Mexico.

You will need:
  1 heavy plastic bag
  1 baking sheet
  1 rolling pin
  1 mixing bowl
  1 mixer or large wooden spoon
  Measuring cup
  Measuring spoons
  Hot pads
  1 spatula
  Wire rack
  1 small bowl or plate

  $^1/_2$ cup butter (1 stick), at room temperature
  1 cup powdered sugar
  2 cups flour
  1 cup pine nuts, or prechopped pecans or walnuts
  2 teaspoons vanilla extract
  $^1/_2$ cup powdered sugar to roll cookies in

What to do:
1. Place prechopped nuts in a heavy plastic bag and crush them with a rolling pin until finely ground.
2. Preheat the oven to 350°.
3. In a large mixing bowl, combine butter, 1 cup powdered sugar, flour, nuts, and vanilla extract.
4. Form the dough into 1-inch balls and place on baking sheet.

5. Bake for 10 to 15 minutes, or until cookies are lightly browned. Using hot pads, remove the baking sheet from the oven and place on a wire rack to cool slightly. Use the spatula to remove cookies from the baking sheet.

6. Place $^1/_2$ cup powdered sugar in a small bowl or on a plate. Roll the baked cookies in the powdered sugar while still warm You may need to roll the cookies twice so they are completely covered in powdered sugar.

 Coyote hint: *Leave the butter unrefrigerated for a few hours until it is at room temperature; this will make it easy to mix with the other ingredients. If the butter doesn't blend well, let it warm on the counter for a little longer. Be sure to cover the butter while it is coming to room temperature.*

 Coyote caution: *Have an adult coyote check the cookies to be sure they are cool enough to handle before trying to roll them in powdered sugar.*

NEW MEXICO NOTE:
The official state animal of New Mexico is the black bear. Did you know the *real* Smokey the Bear was from New Mexico?

Fiesta Fondue

Beginner

These dessert nachos are fun to share. Place toppings in bowls and set them in the center of the table. Serve nacho strips to each person, dip the strips into your favorite topping, and eat.

You will need:
    1 baking sheet
    1 sharp knife
    1 small bowl
    1 fork
    Nonstick vegetable cooking spray
    Small bowls for the toppings
    Measuring cup
    Tablespoon
    Hot pads
    1 spatula

    $^1/_2$ cup sugar
    1 tablespoon ground cinnamon
    8 flour tortillas
    Toppings of your choice: chocolate syrup, caramel syrup,
        whipped cream, thawed frozen strawberries, and so on

What to do:
1. Preheat the oven to 400°.
2. In a small bowl mix together the sugar and cinnamon thoroughly with a fork.
3. Cut the tortillas into strips and place on a baking sheet.
4. Spray the tortilla strips with nonstick vegetable cooking spray.
5. Sprinkle the strips with cinnamon sugar.

6. Bake for 5 to 10 minutes, or until the strips are crispy. Using hot pads, remove the baking sheet from the oven.
7. Using a spatula, remove the strips from the baking sheet to serving plates and let cool for a few minutes.
8. Dip the strips in your favorite topping and eat.

Coyote caution: *Be sure to remove the tortilla strips from the baking sheet with a spatula or fork, as they will be very hot.*

Day of the Dead Bread

FINGER FOOD; MAKES 1 LOAF

Intermediate

November 2 is the Day of the Dead, a Mexican celebration similar to our Halloween. Bread formed into the shape of crossbones is traditionally served.

You will need:
    1 baking sheet
    Shortening to grease the baking sheet
    1 pastry brush
    Measuring spoons
    Hot pads
    1 spatula
    Wire rack
    1 bread knife

    1 teaspoon cornmeal
    2 loaves frozen bread dough, thawed
    1 egg, lightly beaten
    2 tablespoons sugar mixed with 1 teaspoon ground
        cinnamon

What to do:

1. Preheat the oven to 350°.
2. Using a pastry brush, grease a baking sheet with shortening. Sprinkle the cornmeal over the baking sheet.
3. Knead one thawed bread loaf and form into a round loaf. Place it on the baking sheet.
4. Divide the second loaf into fourths. Take one fourth and form the dough into a bone. Place the bone on the round loaf, form another fourth into a second bone and make crossbones on the round loaf.
5. Add the sugar and cinnamon mixture to the lightly beaten egg and brush the bread with this mixture.
6. Place the baking sheet in the oven and bake for 30 minutes, or until the bread is golden brown and sounds hollow when you tap it.
7. Using hot pads, remove the baking sheet from the oven. Using a spatula, carefully transfer the bread to a wire rack to cool.
8. Slice the bread with a bread knife and serve.

 Coyote hint: *Form any leftover dough into 1-inch balls, and let dough balls rise until they double in size. Bake in a 375° oven for 15 minutes or until browned.*

Piñata

Beginner

The traditional *piñata* is made from papier-mâché, but it takes a long time to make and can be hard to break. This version is fast and easy.

You will need:

> 1 brown paper bag, grocery size
> for a large piñata, lunch size
> for a small one
> White glue
> Crepe paper in assorted colors
> Scissors
> Stapler
> Construction paper in assorted
> colors
> Yarn or string
>
> Candy, treats, and small toys

NEW MEXICO NOTE:
The *piñata* was brought to New Mexico by our Mexican neighbors. The *piñata* is filled with toys and candy and hung from a tree or doorway. Children gather around. One child is usually blindfolded and given a stick. He or she swings the stick at the *piñata*. When the *piñata* is broken, the candy and toys are scattered over the area. Children run to retrieve their goodies. *Piñata*s come in many shapes and sizes. This game is often played at birthday parties and during the holidays.

What to do:

1. Put the treats and toys you have inside of the brown paper bag. Staple the top of the sack down so the treats won't spill out.
2. Decide what animal or design you want, and pick crepe paper.
3. Cut the crepe paper into strips. Roll up each strip and cut a fringe along the bottom of each rolled strip. Open up the crepe paper and you will have a long fringe.

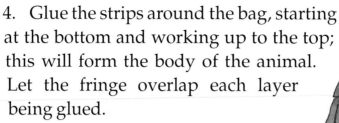

4. Glue the strips around the bag, starting at the bottom and working up to the top; this will form the body of the animal. Let the fringe overlap each layer being glued.

5. Make the head, eyes, and so on out of construction paper and glue them to the top of the paper bag.

6. Staple the yarn to the sack so that the piñata can be hung from a doorway or a tree.

Cornhusk Dolls

Intermediate

CRAFT; MAKES 4 DOLLS

Both boys and girls have been making these dolls for many, many years. Cornhusks can be purchased in the Mexican food section of most grocery stores.

You will need:
1 large bowl
Water
Paper towels
4 large cotton balls
24 cornhusks
Yarn or string
Scissors
Markers, if desired

What to do:
1. Place the cornhusks in a large bowl and cover them with water. Let them

soak for about an hour, until the husks are soft and pliable. Remove the cornhusks from the water and dry with paper towels.

2. Lay one cornhusk flat and place a cotton ball in the center; fold the cornhusk over the cotton ball and twist to form the head of the doll. Tie the neck with string.

3. Take a second cornhusk and roll it up tight so that it is the width of a pencil. Tie each end with string; this will make the doll's arms.

4. Place the arm cornhusk horizontally under the head string. Tie the 2 cornhusks together under the arms to form the doll's waist.

5. Tie 4 or more husks (more will make a larger doll) around the waist to make the bottom of the doll.

6. Draw a face on the doll with markers, if desired.

 Coyote caution: *Be careful when using scissors to cut the string.*

Cody Coyote and the Search for the Indian Diamonds

One night long ago, before the stars had their twinkle, Cody Coyote stood on top of a red Arizona mesa where the sky spirits were known to gather. It was very dark. As Cody watched, the spirits began to work their magic. The North star was the brightest, and the first star that was placed. Next, the Big Dipper was carefully arranged. As usual, Cody could not bear to just sit there and watch; he humbly asked one of the spirits to give him a chance to place some stars. The next thing he knew, he was rising up into the darkness. A buckskin pouch appeared around one shoulder. He reached into the pouch and found that there were beautiful blue stones inside. One by one, Cody carefully offered stones to the sky. Once they were placed, he named the new constellations. Since coyotes were not known for thinking much about anything besides food, he soon was bored with the tedious work.

Frustrated, Cody grabbed the pouch of blue stones and flung its contents across the vast sky. He was pleased; now stars lit up the darkness enough for him to see a lizard hiding under some bushes, snickering. "Why are you laughing at me?" demanded Cody. "Well," said Lizard, "I can't help but think it's terribly funny that you just threw away so many Indian diamonds." Lizard explained to Cody that the blue stones he had flung away were actually valuable turquoise. Realizing he had just made a huge mistake, Cody asked Lizard if he would help him find more

turquoise. "I will help you," said Lizard, "but we will have to go down to the pueblo to find them." "Hop on my back, Lizard," said Cody, "And we'll be on our way."

Cody knew the pueblo people would have plenty of excellent grub to share, and as usual, he was hungry. The pueblo wasn't far, and soon Cody and Lizard were creeping around the adobe houses. The first thing they found were strange clay mounds behind each dwelling. "I smell food!" declared Cody. "Those mounds are ovens, called *hornos*," whispered Lizard. Cody could already smell the bread baking deep inside, and feel the heat from the fire.

"I think I'll have a little Pueblo Bread for my dinner," he said. Lizard retrieved a loaf of bread cooling on one of the window sills for Cody. *"Bewohn o'buyong navi ghe'ma,"* said Lizard, which is what the Isleta people say for "eat well, my friend." Coyote ate almost all of one loaf and burped happily. He tied the remaining piece into his bandanna. With dinner taken care of, Lizard led Cody to a prairie dog town in a field at the edge of the pueblo. Lizard had heard some humans talking of the Indian diamonds, and how prairie dogs liked to hide them in their burrows.

Cody began scratching at the entrance of Prairie Dog's home.

"What's all the racket up there?" yelled Prairie Dog as he peeked out of his tunnel. His social skills were a bit rusty, as he very seldom had visitors. "We're looking for Indian diamonds, but can't seem to find any," said Coyote and Lizard in unison. "Can you tell us where they are?" "Ha ha ha," chuckled Prairie Dog. He was laughing because he had many turquoise stones hidden in his burrow. "I might know where some are," he said, "but I'm gonna need a large piece of that Pueblo Bread to help me remember." "Fine," said Cody, "We'll trade you a piece of bread for the diamonds." As soon as he got his bread, Prairie Dog brought out a large turquoise stone.

Cody put the beautiful stone on a string and tied it around his neck. He looked very grand wearing the turquoise. He liked it so much, in fact, that Cody did not want to share this fortune with Lizard.

His mind started to work quickly. Surely he could outsmart Lizard, and then the Indian diamond would be his alone. But Lizard was no fool. When Cody began to slink away, Lizard became very angry. "I want my share of the Indian diamonds!" yelled Lizard. Cody started to run, but Lizard was right behind him. Just as Cody was about to get away, Lizard jumped up and bit Cody's tail. "YEOOOOOOW!" yipped Cody. He was shocked; he shook and shook his tail so hard that Lizard was thrown clear to the next mesa. But now his sleek tail was puffed out bigger than a hot-air balloon! And that is why to this very day, Coyote has a puffy tail.

Native American Recipes

Cactus Cooler

Beginner

This sherbet soda really looks like cactus juice! It's cool and refreshing.

You will need:
  4 tall glasses
  1 ice cream scoop
  Measuring cup

  1 bottle lemon-lime soda (1-liter size)
  4 scoops lime sherbet
  Straw
  Spoon

What to do:
1. Pour 1 cup of lemon-lime soda into each glass.
2. Place a scoop of lime sherbet carefully into each glass. Serve with a straw and a spoon.

ARIZONA ANSWER: Speaking of cactus, the saguaro cactus can be found only in the Sonoran Desert. These giant cactus may grow to be 50 feet tall and weigh as much as 8 tons—although it may take them 150 years to get that big.

Papago Pumpkin

Intermediate

This tastes sort of like pumpkin pie, only better! Why not buy an extra pumpkin at Halloween this year and make this super dessert?

You will need:
   1 baking dish
   1 serrated steak knife
   Measuring cup
   Measuring spoons
   Hot pads
   Serving spoon

   2 cups peeled, cubed pumpkin
   $2/3$ cup brown sugar
   1 tablespoon melted butter
   Whipped cream

What to do:
1. Preheat the oven to 350°.
2. Place pumpkin cubes in a baking dish.
3. Sprinkle the brown sugar over the pumpkin cubes; then drizzle melted butter over the sugar.
4. Bake for 30 minutes, or until the pumpkin is tender when you stick it with a fork.
5. Using hot pads, carefully remove the baking dish from the oven.
6. Spoon the pumpkin into bowls and serve with whipped cream.

Coyote caution: *Have an adult coyote cut the pumpkin into cubes. If the pumpkin is difficult to cut and peel, bake the whole pumpkin at 350° for 30 to 40 minutes, let cool, and then peel and cube for the recipe.*

Prairie Dog Pumpkin Muffins

FINGER FOOD; MAKES ABOUT 12 MUFFINS

Advanced

Pumpkins are an American original. Native Americans did not waste any part of the pumpkin. The seeds were roasted and saved for the winter, and the shells were even used for bowls!

You will need:

1 muffin tin
Cupcake papers
2 mixing bowls
Wooden spoon
Measuring cups and spoons
Hot pads
Wire rack

1 1/2 cups brown sugar
1 cup canned pumpkin
1/2 cup vegetable oil
1/2 cup water
2 eggs
1 2/3 cups flour
1/2 teaspoon baking powder
1 teaspoon baking soda
1/2 teaspoon salt
1 teaspoon ground cinnamon
1/2 teaspoon ground nutmeg
1/4 teaspoon ground cloves
1/2 cup piñon nuts, toasted and chopped, or substitute your
    favorite nut (optional)

ARIZONA ANSWER:
The Grand Canyon is located in Northern Arizona and is 1 mile deep and 280 miles long. It took more than 6 million years for the Grand Canyon to be formed by the flow of the Colorado River.

What to do:

1. Preheat the oven to 400°.
2. In a mixing bowl, thoroughly combine the sugar, pumpkin, oil, water, and eggs.
3. In the other mixing bowl, stir together the flour, baking powder, baking soda, salt, cinnamon, nutmeg, and cloves. Stir in the nuts.
4. Slowly stir the flour mixture into the pumpkin mixture. Blend well.
5. Place a cupcake paper in each muffin cup. Spoon the pumpkin batter into the muffin cups, filling them two-thirds full.
6. Place muffin tin in oven and bake for 20 to 25 minutes, or until lightly browned.
7. Using hot pads, remove muffin tin from oven and let cool on a wire rack.

Roadrunner Roasted Piñon Nuts

FINGER FOOD; MAKES 1 CUP

Intermediate

Piñons are also known as pine nuts. They are usually located in the nut and candy section of your grocery store.

You will need:
1 baking pan
Spoon or fork
Measuring cup
Hot pads

1 cup unshelled or shelled piñon or pine nuts

What to do:

1. Preheat the oven to 300°.
2. Rinse off the nuts. Place them in one layer in a baking pan.
3. Place baking pan in oven and bake for 1 hour, stirring every 10 minutes so the nuts brown evenly. When stirring, use hot pads to remove the pan from the oven, and to hold the pan while you stir the nuts.
4. Using hot pads, remove the baking pan from the oven and let the nuts cool. Remove the nuts from the baking pan and store in a plastic bag.

 Coyote caution: *Let the nuts cool before removing them from the baking pan and storing them in plastic bags.*

 Coyote hint: *In case piñons come with shells in your part of the world, here's a way to remove the nuts from their shells. Place a dish towel on the counter. Spread the warm nuts over the towel, then cover them with a second towel. Rub the nuts to remove the shells, then pick out the "meat" from inside. If this doesn't work, lightly tap the nuts with a small rock—but be gentle; you don't want to crush the nuts.*

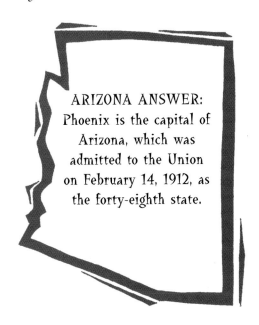

ARIZONA ANSWER: Phoenix is the capital of Arizona, which was admitted to the Union on February 14, 1912, as the forty-eighth state.

Powerful Piñons

Intermediate

Every fall Native American families go collecting the delicious piñons. They clean them, roast them, and keep them to snack on during the winter. For a real zing, give these Powerful Piñons a try; they've got just enough chili powder on them to be fun!

You will need:

1 baking sheet
Nonstick vegetable cooking spray
Measuring cup
Measuring spoons
Hot pads

1 cup piñon nuts, roasted and shelled (see the Roadrunner Roasted Piñon Nuts recipe, page 62)
$1/8$ teaspoon chili powder

What to do:
1. Preheat the oven to 300°.
2. Spread the roasted nuts evenly on a baking sheet.
3. Spray the nuts lightly with nonstick vegetable cooking spray and sprinkle with chili powder.
4. Bake for 5 to 10 minutes, until the nuts are heated through.
5. Using hot pads, remove the baking sheet from the oven and let the nuts cool. Store the cooled nuts in a plastic bag.

Coyote caution: *Be careful to sprinkle the red chili powder evenly and lightly. If you don't like hot food, cut back on the amount of chili powder.*

Intermediate

Leapin' Lizard Leather

FINGER FOOD; MAKES 4 SMALL FRUIT ROLLS OR 1 LARGE ONE

This lizard leather bears no resemblance to the skin of the Gila monster, one of the biggest and most poisonous lizards in the world, which happens to call Arizona home. Don't worry; the plastic wrap in this recipe won't melt at a low temperature.

You will need:
    1 large baking sheet
    Plastic wrap
    1 serrated steak knife
    1 blender
    Measuring cup
    Hot pads

    $1^1/_2$ cups very ripe chopped fruit (try kiwi—it's green!)
    $^1/_4$ cup light corn syrup

What to do:
1. Place the chopped fruit and the corn syrup in a blender and purée. The purée should be smooth, without any lumps.
2. Place plastic wrap over the baking sheet and pour the purée onto it. Smooth the purée so that it covers the baking sheet evenly. (The mixture should be thin, about $^1/_8$ inch thick.)
3. Put the baking sheet in a warm oven, 140°, for 4 to 6 hours, checking it every half hour. Dry the purée until it is pliable and has the feel of leather. It shouldn't be wet or very sticky.
4. Using hot pads, remove the baking sheet from the oven, let the leather cool, and then roll it up in the plastic wrap.

Coyote caution: *Check the fruit leather every half hour, as different fruits dry at different speeds.*

Pueblo "Horno" Bread

FINGER FOOD; MAKES 2 LOAVES

Advanced

Native Americans use small adobe ovens located outside of their homes to bake bread. They make fires in these ovens and then bake the bread. These ancient outdoor adobe ovens, or "hornos" as they are called, are still used today by Native Americans.

You will need:

    1 baking sheet
    Pastry brush and shortening to grease the baking sheet
    1 cooking thermometer
    1 or 2 large mixing bowls
    1 large mixing spoon or wooden spoon
    Floured surface
    1 damp cloth
    Measuring cups
    Measuring spoons
    Hot pads
    1 spatula
    Wire rack

    1 package dry yeast
    $1/3$ cup warm water (125°)
    2 tablespoons melted butter
    1 teaspoon salt
    4 to 5 cups all-purpose flour
    1 cup water

ARIZONA ANSWER:
Just as an oven gets hot, things sure do heat up in Arizona! The record high in the state is 127 degrees Fahrenheit.

What to do:

1. Using the pastry brush, brush shortening evenly and lightly over the baking sheet and set aside.

2. Place warm water (temperature should be 125°) in a large mixing bowl with the yeast, stir to dissolve, and let the yeast rest for a few minutes.

3. Add the melted butter and salt to the yeast. Slowly stir in a little of the flour, then a little of the water, then flour, then water until a dough is formed.

4. Remove the dough from the bowl and knead it on a floured surface (fold and press the dough as you would clay). Keep kneading until the dough is smooth. This may take 10 minutes or so.

5. Shape the dough into a ball and place it in a large bowl. If you use the same bowl you used to mix the dough, wash it out first. Cover the bowl with a damp cloth. Let the dough rise in the bowl until is doubled in size (about 1½ hours).

6. Punch the dough; it will fall. Remove the dough from the bowl and knead it on a floured surface for a minute. Divide the dough in half, and shape each half into a round loaf. Set the loaves on the greased baking sheet and let them rise for 20 minutes. Preheat the oven to 400° while they are rising.

7. Place the baking sheet in the oven and bake for 45 to 50 minutes, or until the loaves are browned.

8. Using hot pads, remove the baking sheet from the oven. Use a spatula to move the loaves to a wire rack to cool.

 Coyote hint: *Be sure to use a thermometer to measure the temperature of water before you add the yeast. If it's too hot it will kill the yeast and the bread won't rise; if it's too cool the yeast won't activate and the bread won't rise.*

A-Maizeing Corn

FINGER FOOD; MAKES 4 SERVINGS

Intermediate

Maize is the Indian word for corn. Traditionally, dried corn kernels were placed on a grinding stone and ground into meal or flour.

You will need:
>   1 charcoal grill
>   Long-handled tongs
>   1 large tub of water or sink of water
>   Hot pads
>
>   4 ears corn, with the husks on but tassels removed
>   Butter
>   Salt and pepper

What to do:
1. Soak the ears of corn in water for 4 to 6 hours.
2. Have an adult coyote start the grill. When it is hot, remove the corn from the water, pat it dry, and place it on the grill.
3. Let the corn grill for 5 minutes, turn it a quarter turn, using long-handled tongs, and cook for 5 minutes more. Continue until the corn is browned on all sides.
4. Use long-handled tongs to remove the corn to a plate. Holding the corn with a hot pad, pull back and remove the husks. Serve the corn with butter, salt, and pepper. The corn will be taffy colored, and the kernels will be lightly browned.

Coyote caution: *Be sure to handle hot corn with tongs and hot pads.*

Coyote hint: *If a grill is not available, roast the corn in a 350° oven for 10 to 15 minutes. You can also place it in campfire coals for 20 minutes.*

Intermediate

Powwow Posole

This stew is made with hominy, a type of corn. To make your own flour tortillas to go with it, see page 34. Did you know that Indian corn comes in colors like white, red, blue, and even black?

You will need:

>   1 large saucepan
>   1 sharp knife
>   1 large wooden spoon
>   Measuring cup
>   Measuring spoons
>   Hot pads
>   Ladle

>   1 tablespoon margarine or vegetable shortening
>   1 pound lean pork, cut into $1/2$-inch cubes
>   4 cups water
>   2 cups canned hominy
>   1 teaspoon salt
> $1/4$ to $1/2$ teaspoon chili powder

What to do:

1. In a large saucepan over medium heat, melt the margarine. Add the pork and fry, stirring occasionally, until browned.
2. Add the water, hominy, and salt. Simmer uncovered for 2 hours on the lowest heat. Stir the posole every 10 to 20 minutes to prevent sticking and burning.
3. Add chili powder to taste. Ladle the posole into bowls and serve with flour tortillas.

 Coyote caution: *Use hot pads to hold the saucepan while stirring.*

Chaco Tacos

Intermediate

These tacos are an adaptation of a Native American food. They are traditionally made with Indian fry bread. We've substituted bread rounds here because fry bread is difficult to obtain or make.

You will need:

4 microwave-safe serving plates
Serving spoons
Grater
1 serrated steak knife
1 large frying pan
1 large spoon
Measuring cup
Tablespoon
Hot pads

1 pound extra-lean ground beef
$^1/_4$ cup salsa
4 small bread rounds (such as Boboli brand) or small
    pita rounds
1 can (16 ounces) refried beans
1 cup grated Colby cheese
1 cup shredded iceberg lettuce
1 small tomato, chopped
Salsa or green chile sauce (optional)

What to do:

1. In a large frying pan, brown and crumble the ground beef, cooking it until it is thoroughly brown and there is no pink. Stir in the salsa. Remove the pan from the heat and set aside.

2. Place one of the bread rounds on each serving plate.
3. Spread 2 tablespoons of refried beans on each bread round. Spoon one fourth of the meat mixture on top of the beans. Sprinkle one-fourth cup of the cheese on top of the rounds.
4. Place one of the plates in the microwave and microwave on high for 1 minute. Using hot pads, carefully remove the plate from the microwave. Repeat with the remaining plates. Top each round with one fourth of the lettuce and one fourth of the tomatoes. If desired, top with salsa or chile sauce.

 Coyote caution: *Always use hot pads when removing dishes from the microwave; sometimes the dishes can become hot. Chaco Tacos are meant to be eaten with a knife and fork.*

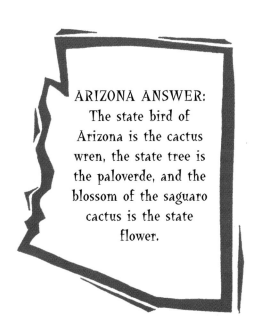

ARIZONA ANSWER:
The state bird of Arizona is the cactus wren, the state tree is the paloverde, and the blossom of the saguaro cactus is the state flower.

Full Moon Pudding

DESSERT; MAKES 12 SERVINGS

Advanced

This dish is traditional to Pueblo Native Americans; they call it pudding. It tastes like pumpkin pie filling, but it's made with cornmeal.

You will need:

1 large saucepan
Small bowl and fork, for beating the eggs
1 wooden spoon
Nonstick vegetable cooking spray
9 x 9-inch or 10 x 10-inch square baking pan
Measuring cups
Measuring spoons
Hot pads

3 cups milk
$1/2$ cup molasses or dark corn syrup
$1/3$ cup cornmeal
2 eggs, lightly beaten
2 tablespoons butter
$1/2$ teaspoon ground ginger
$1/2$ teaspoon ground cinnamon
$1/2$ teaspoon ground nutmeg
$1/8$ teaspoon salt
Whipped cream (optional)

What to do:

1. Preheat the oven to 325°.
2. In a large saucepan, over medium heat, stir together the milk and molasses and heat until hot but not boiling.

3. Slowly stir in the cornmeal. Cook and stir until the mixture thickens, and then remove the pan from the heat.
4. Stir in the eggs and butter; then add the ginger, cinnamon, nutmeg, and salt. Stir until well blended.
5. Spray the baking pan with nonstick vegetable cooking spray, and pour the mixture into the pan.
6. Place the pan in the oven and bake for 1 hour and 15 minutes.
7. Using hot pads, remove the pudding from the oven and let cool. You can serve it warm or cool. Cut it into squares and serve with whipped cream, if you like.

 Coyote caution: *Be sure to remove the cornmeal mixture from the heat as soon as it thickens to prevent burning and to keep the mixture from splattering.*

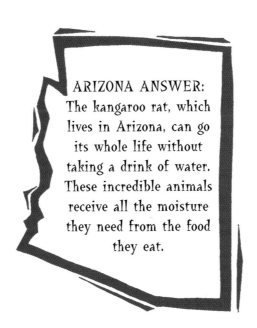

ARIZONA ANSWER: The kangaroo rat, which lives in Arizona, can go its whole life without taking a drink of water. These incredible animals receive all the moisture they need from the food they eat.

Indian Diamonds

Intermediate

These cookies are as blue as the beautiful skies over Arizona. They may even turn your tongue blue when you eat them!

You will need:

    1 baking sheet
    Nonstick vegetable cooking spray
    1 large mixing bowl
    1 wooden mixing spoon
    Measuring cups
    Measuring spoons
    1 rolling pin
    Floured surface
    1 diamond-shaped cookie cutter
    Hot pads
    1 spatula
    Wire rack

    1 cup shortening
    2 cups sugar
    2 eggs
    1 teaspoon vanilla extract
    Few drops blue or turquoise food coloring
    2 teaspoons baking powder
    3 cups flour
    1/2 cup milk
    Sugar for sprinkling on the cookies

What to do:

1. Preheat the oven to 350°. Spray a baking sheet with nonstick vegetable cooking spray.

2. In a large bowl, beat together the shortening and sugar. Blend in eggs, then vanilla extract, food coloring, baking powder, and flour. Add milk and mix until a dough is formed.

3. Place the dough on a floured surface. With a rolling pin, roll the dough out to a thickness of $1/2$ inch. Using a diamond cookie cutter, cut out diamond cookies and place them on the baking sheet. Lightly sprinkle the cookies with sugar.

4. Place the baking sheet in the oven and bake for 15 minutes, or until the "diamonds" are lightly browned. Using hot pads, remove the baking sheet from the oven. Using a spatula, carefully remove the cookies to a wire rack to cool. Roll out, cut, and bake the remaining dough, gathering up the dough scraps and rerolling them as needed.

 Coyote hint: *If the dough is hard to mix and you have permission, use an electric mixer to blend the cookie ingredients together.*

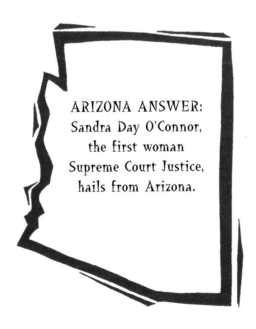

ARIZONA ANSWER:
Sandra Day O'Connor,
the first woman
Supreme Court Justice,
hails from Arizona.

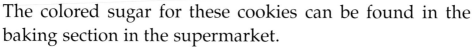

Sandpainted Suns

DESSERT; MAKES 12 SUNS OR 4 SERVINGS

Intermediate

The colored sugar for these cookies can be found in the baking section in the supermarket.

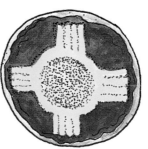

You will need:

    Waxed paper
    1 butter knife
    Small bowl to mix frosting in
    Small bowls to hold colored sugar
    1 mixing spoon

    12 large, round baked sugar cookies
    1 container white prepared frosting
    Yellow food coloring
    Sugar in assorted colors

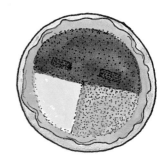

What to do:

1. Place waxed paper over your work area. Place the frosting in a mixing bowl, add 5 or 6 drops of yellow food coloring, and stir with a mixing spoon until the frosting is yellow and the color is even. If the yellow is not dark enough, add a few more drops of food coloring and mix well.
2. With a knife, frost each cookie with a thin layer of frosting.
3. Make Native American-style designs on your yellow "sun" cookies by carefully sprinkling the colored sugar onto them. The sugars will replace the sand used in Native American art. Or try making pictures of corn stalks and chiles.

Coyote hint: *You can also make a stencil out of paper, place it on a frosted cookie, and then sprinkle sugar over it. Carefully remove the stencil and your design will be on the cookie!*

Gourd Dance Rattles

Beginner

Gourds played an important part in the everyday lives of Native Americans. In addition to being used as rattles for ceremonial dances, they were made into spoons, dippers, and small bowls. In the fall you can find dried gourds in the produce section of most grocery stores.

You will need:
    Sheets of plastic or waxed paper to cover work surface
    Paper towel
    4 dried gourds (choose gourds that have a long neck that can
        be used as a handle)
    Assortment of acrylic paints
    Paintbrushes
    Empty egg cartons to dry gourds

What to do:
1. Cover your work surface with sheets of plastic or waxed paper to catch any paint drips.
2. Rinse and dry the gourds with a paper towel.
3. Paint Native American-style designs on the gourds; set the gourds aside on empty egg cartons until the paint has dried.

 Coyote caution: *Always paint in a well-ventilated area so the fumes won't bother you.*

 Coyote hint: *If you can't find dried gourds with seeds that rattle, purchase freshly picked gourds and let them dry until they rattle. (This may take a few weeks.) Turn the gourds daily to prevent spoilage and molding.*

Indian Coil Pottery

CRAFT; MAKES 4 OR MORE POTTERY BOWLS,
DEPENDING ON THE SIZE OF THE PIECES

Advanced This pottery is the perfect place to keep your special things, such as neat rocks or leaves, or even a necklace or ring!

You will need:

1 baking sheet
Nonstick vegetable cooking spray
1 large mixing bowl
1 large wooden spoon
Assortment of acrylic paints
Paintbrushes
Hot pads
Clear acrylic spray

2 cups flour
$1/2$ cup salt
$1/2$ teaspoon cream of tartar
$2/3$ cup water

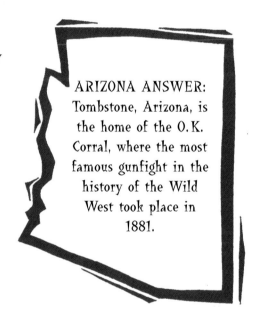

ARIZONA ANSWER:
Tombstone, Arizona, is the home of the O.K. Corral, where the most famous gunfight in the history of the Wild West took place in 1881.

What to do:

1. In a large mixing bowl, combine the flour, salt, and cream of tartar. Mix in the water until well blended.
2. Knead the clay with your hands. If it feels too dry, add a little more water; if it feels wet, add a little more flour. It should be the consistency of clay.
3. Roll the clay into long, snakelike strips.
4. Take one strip and coil it to make a flat base for the bowl.

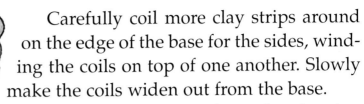

Carefully coil more clay strips around on the edge of the base for the sides, winding the coils on top of one another. Slowly make the coils widen out from the base.

Smooth out the sides of your bowl, using a little bit of water and your hands, so the edges are smooth and the coils are sealed together.

5. Spray a baking sheet with nonstick vegetable cooking spray and place the bowl on it. Place the baking sheet in a warm oven, 140° to 150°, and let the bowl dry for 6 to 8 hours. Using hot pads, remove the baking sheet from the oven to cool. When the bowl is cool and dry, paint it with Native American-style designs. To finish the pottery, you can spray it with clear acrylic spray.

 Coyote hint: *For a subtle color in your pottery, add a few drops of food coloring to some of the clay. Experiment with different colors and paints for a southwestern look.*

 Coyote caution: *Never use acrylic spray indoors. Always spray outside or in a well-vented area.*

 Coyote caution: *These pots are strictly for decoration. They will fall apart if they are placed in a hot oven; do not use them to bake food.*

Cody Coyote's Favorite Menus

New Mexican Fiesta

Many New Mexican dishes are made even better by the addition of the super sauces and salsas that make New Mexican food such spicy fun.

Bunch o' Muncho Nachos
Sizzlin' Sombreros
Burros
Feast Day Cookies

Serve with sides of Hotter than You-Know-What Salsa or Holy Moly Guacamole.

Cowboy Cookout

These rustic recipes will fill up even the hungriest of hombres after a long day's ride.

Sidewinder Sausages
Campfire Fries
Howlin' Coyote Toast
Tall Texas Tea
Rocky Mountain Mud Pie

Native American Powwow

This is an authentic Native American menu which would likely be a part of a powwow or gathering in Arizona, Colorado, New Mexico, Texas, or Utah. Native Americans have many special gatherings for important events such as the changing of the seasons, harvests, or religious ceremonies.

Chaco Taco
A-Maizeing Corn
Pueblo Horno Bread
Full Moon Pudding

Glossary

adobe: A mud and straw mixture used to make houses, ovens, and other things such as fences.

bandanna: A colorful scarf worn by cowboys.

bewohn o' buyong, navi ghe' ma: A phrase from the Islete Indian language meaning "eat well, my friend."

burrito: A tortilla wrapped around beans, meat, or other filling.

champurro: The Spanish word for hot chocolate.

constellation: Stars lined up to look like a picture. The Big Dipper is made up of a constellation of stars.

cuisine: A manner of preparing food or a style of cooking.

culture: The concepts, habits, skills, arts, foods, and institutions of a given people.

empanada: This word is taken from the Spanish term *empanaris,* which means "to bake in pastry." This special pastry is usually filled with savory meat or vegetables, but can also be filled with fruit or even chocolate.

fiesta: A party or celebration in a Mexican village or New Mexican town. Many times there is music and dancing during this special event. The whole village pitches in to prepare food for the feast that is shared.

horno: An outdoor oven made of adobe that is used to baked bread at many Native American homes on the pueblo.

mariachi: A small band of musicians that plays wonderful Mexican music. The band often walks around while it plays and is made up of trumpets, guitars, and violins.

mesa: A small, high plateau or flat tableland with steep sides and, often, a layer of rock covering it.

muy importante: A Spanish phrase meaning "very important."

nachos: A great New Mexican snack of tortillas, cheese, and salsa.

piñata: A clay or papier-mâché container of various forms and shapes, hung from the ceiling on a special day and broken in a game by children with a stick so as to release the candy and toys inside. This is a traditional activity from Mexico that has been eagerly adopted by children from around the world.

piñons: Also known as pine nuts, these are little brown nuts found on piñon trees, which are found at higher elevations in the Southwest. They are often gathered in the fall and roasted.

pueblo: A type of village found among southwestern Native Americans. Pueblos are often made up of ancient adobe houses connected together like apartments or town houses.

siesta: The Spanish word for nap.

sombrero: A large hat, made of straw, felt, or velvet, worn by men in Mexico to protect them from the hot sun.

tradition: A practice, statement, opinion, or belief handed down from one generation to another.